GIGANOTOSAURUS

A Buddy **Book**
by
Michael P. Goecke

ABDO
Publishing Company

VISIT US AT

www.abdopublishing.com

Published by ABDO Publishing Company, 4940 Viking Drive, Edina, Minnesota 55435.

Printed in the United States.

Edited by: Sarah Tieck
Graphic Design: Denise Esner
Cover Art: Natural History Museum, title page
Interior Photos/Illustrations: Pages 5 & 8: Bruno Hernandez; pages 6 & 7 Joe Tucciarone; page 11: Photos.com; pages 13, 14, 19 & 24: Natural History Museum; page 17: Luis Rey; page 21: John Sibbick; page 23: Pro Litho; page 25: American Museum of Natural History; page 26: Getty Images.

Library of Congress Cataloging-in-Publication Data

Goecke, Michael P., 1968-
    Giganotosaurus / Michael P. Goecke.
        p. cm. (Dinosaurs)
    Includes index.
    ISBN-13: 978-1-59928-697-6
    ISBN-10: 1-59928-697-1
        1. Giganotosaurus—Juvenile literature. I. Title.

    QE862.S3G644 2007
    567.912—dc22

                                                    2006031465

ABLE OF CONTENTS

WHAT WAS IT?

Millions of years ago, Earth was a very different place. Dinosaurs walked the earth. Some of them were as big as buildings. Others were as small as chickens.

The Giganotosaurus was a large, **carnivorous** dinosaur. It may have weighed more than 16,000 pounds (7,000 kg). That is as heavy as five hippopotamuses!

One Giganotosaurus skeleton that was found measured about 45 feet (14 m) long. And, it was almost 17 feet (5 m) tall!

Giganotosaurus
jee-guh-NOH-toh-sawr-uhs

Scientists know that the Giganotosaurus walked on its strong legs.

TAIL

But, they disagree about how fast it moved.

The Giganotosaurus had lighter bones than most large **carnivores**. Some scientists believe this may have helped it run fast.

LEG

FOOT

HEAD

ARM

Other scientists believe the Giganotosaurus moved more slowly and carefully. They say if it fell, its small arms could not have broken its fall. A fall could have killed it.

But, the Giganotosaurus was a **carnivore**. So, it must have been quick enough to catch other animals for food.

Scientists say the Giganotosaurus is one of the longest **predators** ever discovered. Its **skull** alone was more than five feet (two m) long. That is as big as a bathtub!

The Giganotosaurus was a very large predator.

The Giganotosaurus's mouth was filled with eight-inch (20-cm) long teeth. These teeth were serrated. This means they had little bumps, just like a saw. These bumps helped with cutting.

Inside the Giganotosaurus's large head was a small brain. It was about the size and shape of a banana. Scientists know that a big part of the Giganotosaurus's brain was used for smelling. This may have helped it find food.

LAND OF THE GIGANOTOSAURUS

The Giganotosaurus lived during the Late **Cretaceous period**. It lived about 95 million years ago in what is now Argentina. The climate was warmer then.

During this time, flowering plants called angiosperms became more common. The Giganotosaurus ate herbivorous dinosaurs. These dinosaurs, such as sauropods, probably ate angiosperms.

Maple trees are modern-day angiosperms.

WHAT ELSE LIVED THERE?

The Giganotosaurus lived with many sauropod dinosaurs. Sauropods had long necks and were very large.

Some scientists think that Giganotosaurus dinosaurs might have hunted in groups. This would have made it possible for them to catch huge sauropods.

The Aeolosaurus was a sauropod dinosaur. About 70 million years ago, the Aeolosaurus lived in the same area as the Giganotosaurus.

This sauropod was 50 feet (15 m) long and weighed about 23,000 pounds (10,500 kg). However, scientists can only guess the Aeolosaurus's size. This is because no complete **fossil** has been found.

The Aeolosaurus (ee-O-low-sawr-uhs) was a huge herbivorous, dinosaur.

A sauropod that lived around the same time as the Giganotosaurus was the Antarctosaurus. The Antarctosaurus is one of the largest dinosaurs ever to exist. It was 100 feet (30 m) long. This very big dinosaur may have weighed more than 75,000 pounds (34,000 kg).

Antarctosaurus (ant-ARK-toe-sawr-uhs)

 WHAT DID IT EAT?

Scientists are sure the Giganotosaurus was a **carnivore**. Some say it ate some of the largest dinosaurs ever to exist.

So, how did the Giganotosaurus catch large dinosaurs? Scientists are still exploring what might have happened. They observe modern animals to create **theories** about how dinosaurs might have behaved.

One of the animals that scientists look at is the African lion. African lions work together to hunt animals that are much larger than them.

A single lion weighs about 300 pounds (140 kg). But, a group of lions working together can catch a 2,000 pound (900 kg) Cape buffalo. Like lions, Giganotosaurus dinosaurs could have teamed up to hunt larger dinosaurs, such as the Antarctosaurus.

WHO WERE ITS ENEMIES?

Giganotosaurus dinosaurs may have competed with each other for food.

Because it was so large, the Giganotosaurus probably did not have many enemies. It was big enough to protect itself. But, smaller **predators** may have tried to eat a sick or hurt Giganotosaurus.

17

Scientists are still learning how Giganotosaurus dinosaurs acted around each other. Some think these large dinosaurs worked together in packs. Others think they may have been enemies and fought over food. No one knows for sure.

THE GIGANOTOSAURUS FAMILY

The Giganotosaurus is a theropod. Theropods stood on their back legs and had sharp teeth. This makes the Giganotosaurus a distant relative of the Tyrannosaurus rex. The T. rex is one of the most famous dinosaurs of all.

This T. rex skeleton is in London's Natural History Museum.

Both the Giganotosaurus and the T. rex were **carnivores**. But, the T. rex lived about 30 million years after the Giganotosaurus. And, it lived in parts of what is now North America.

Giganotosaurus is similar in size to the T. rex, but even bigger. Both dinosaurs had big heads and teeth. Also, their arms were much smaller than their legs.

Tyrannosaurus rex means "terrible lizard king."

RAISING ITS YOUNG

Scientists are still working to learn how the Giganotosaurus raised its young. They compare the Giganotosaurus to modern animals to find out information.

Some scientists say theropods, such as the Giganotosaurus, might be the **ancestors** of today's birds. This is because their bones are similar.

Scientists know that the Giganotosaurus laid eggs. They do not know if it built a nest like birds. But, **fossils** of other theropod eggs have been found in nests.

The Giganotosaurus might have built nests for its eggs.

DISCOVERY

The discovery of the Giganotosaurus helped scientists better understand large dinosaur predators.

In 1993, Rubén D. Carolini discovered the first Giganotosaurus **fossils** in Patagonia, Argentina. Searching for fossils was just his hobby. But, this was an important discovery!

Carolini told scientists Rodolfo Coria and Leonardo Salgado about his discovery. They wanted to find more Giganotosaurus **fossils**.

Giganotosaurus fossils were first discovered in Patagonia, Argentina.

Scientists work carefully at an excavation site. They use special tools to remove fossils from the ground.

Coria and Salgado **excavated** the site where Carolini discovered the first **fossils**. Eventually, they found a nearly complete fossil skeleton.

The two scientists named this new **species** Giganotosaurus. The full name is *Giganotosaurus carolini*. The last part of the name is in honor of Rubén D. Carolini, for his discovery.

Carmen Funes Municipal Museum
55° North Cordova Street
National Route 40 and Provincial Route 7
Plaza Huincul, Neuquén, Argentina

GIGANOTOSAURUS

NAME MEANS	Giant southern lizard
DIET	Meat
WEIGHT	16,000 pounds (7,000 kg)
LENGTH	45 feet (14 m)
TIME	Late Cretaceous period
ANOTHER THEROPOD	Tyrannosaurus rex
SPECIAL FEATURE	One of the longest predators
FOSSILS FOUND	Argentina

The Giganotosaurus lived 95 million years ago.

The first humans appeared 1.6 million years ago.

Triassic Period	Jurassic Period	Cretaceous Period	Tertiary Period
245 Million years ago	208 Million years ago	144 Million years ago	65 Million years ago
Mesozoic Era			Cenozoic Era

29

WEB SITES

To learn more about the Giganotosaurus, visit ABDO Publishing Company on the World Wide Web. Web sites about the Giganotosaurus are featured on our "Book Links" page. These links are routinely monitored and updated to provide the most current information available.

www.abdopublishing.com

IMPORTANT WORDS

ancestor a member of a family that lived in the past.

carnivore a meat-eater.

Cretaceous period a period of time that happened 144–65 million years ago.

excavate to carefully dig out material from the ground.

fossil remains of very old animals and plants commonly found in the ground. A fossil can be a bone, a footprint, or any trace of life.

herbivore plant-eater.

predator an animal that hunts and eats other animals.

skull the bony part of the head that protects the brain.

species a group of animals with many things in common.

theory an idea.

INDEX